SO-DZB-909

D1520164

PowerKids Readers:

My World of Science™

Bilingual Edition
English/Spanish
Edición bilingüe

Levers in My World

Palancas en mi mundo

Joanne Randolph

Traducción al español: María Cristina Brusca

The Rosen Publishing Group's
PowerKids Press™ & **Editorial Buenas Letras**™
New York

For Linda Lou and Lucas

Published in 2006 by The Rosen Publishing Group, Inc.
29 East 21st Street, New York, NY 10010

First Edition

Photo Credits: Cover (wheelbarrow) © Randy Miller/Corbis; cover and p. 11 © Thomas J. Peterson/Getty Images; cover and p. 9 © Steve Smith/Getty Images; pp. 5, 22, (fulcrum) © Martin Barraud/Getty Images; pp. 7, 22 (effort), (load) © Reuters/Corbis; p. 13 Cindy Reiman; p. 15 © Anne Ackermann/Getty Images; p. 17 © Ricky John Molloy/Getty Images; p. 19 © Zephyr Picture/Index Stock Imagery, Inc.; p. 21 © Gabe Palmer/Corbis; p. 22 (jack) © Shawn Frederick/Getty Images.

Library of Congress Cataloging-in-Publication Data

Randolph, Joanne.
[Levers in my world. Spanish & English] Levers in my world = Palancas en mi mundo / Joanne Randolph ; traducción al español, María Cristina Brusca.— 1st ed.
p. cm. — (My world of science)
Includes bibliographical references and index. ISBN 1-4042-3321-0
1. Levers—Juvenile literature. I. Title.
TJ147.R29 2006
621.8'11—dc22
2005005973

Manufactured in the United States of America

Contents

Contenido

A lever can be used to lift or move objects. A lever is a simple machine. A simple machine helps people do work.

Una palanca puede utilizarse para levantar o mover objetos. Una palanca es una máquina simple. Las máquinas simples ayudan a la gente a trabajar.

A lever is often a straight board. It moves back and forth on a fixed point called a fulcrum. The load is what you want to lift. You press on the lever to lift the load. This is called effort.

Una barra sirve a menudo como palanca. Se mueve en direcciones opuestas apoyándose en un punto fijo, llamado fulcro. La carga es aquello que quieres levantar. Para levantar la carga presionas la palanca. Esta presión se llama fuerza.

load
carga

fulcrum
fulcro

effort
fuerza

7

A seesaw is a lever. If you sit on a seesaw, you can easily lift another person off the ground. The center of the seesaw is the fulcrum. You and your friend are the load and the effort.

Un subibaja es una palanca. Cuando te sientas en un subibaja, puedes levantar a otra persona del suelo con facilidad. El centro del subibaja es el fulcro. Tu amigo y tú son la carga y la fuerza.

There are three kinds of levers. The first kind is a first-class lever, like a seesaw. The fulcrum is in the middle. The effort and load are at either end. A hammer is a first-class lever, too.

Existen tres tipos de palancas. El primer tipo es la palanca de primer género, como el subibaja. El fulcro está en el medio. La fuerza y la carga están en los dos extremos. El martillo es también una palanca de primer género.

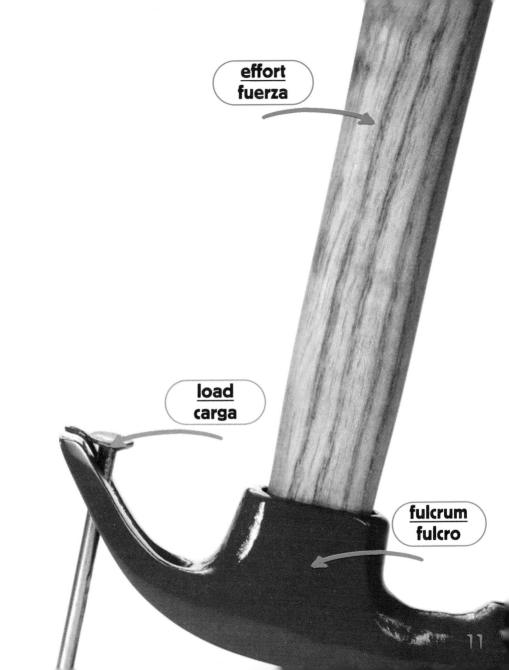

effort
fuerza

load
carga

fulcrum
fulcro

11

A second-class lever has its fulcrum at the end. The load is in the middle. A bottle opener is a second-class lever. The opener makes it easier to lift the cap off a bottle.

La palanca de segundo género tiene el fulcro en un extremo. La carga está en el centro. El destapador de botellas es una palanca de segundo género. El destapador nos ayuda a abrir la tapa de la botella.

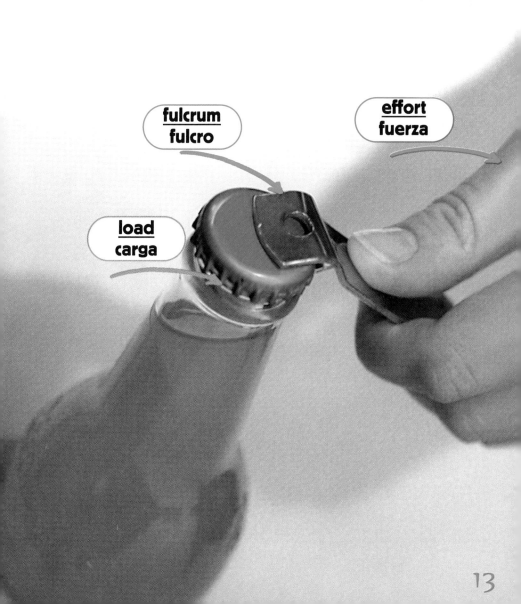

fulcrum
fulcro

effort
fuerza

load
carga

A lever with the fulcrum at one end and the load at the other end is called a third-class lever. In this kind of lever the effort is in the middle. A fishing rod is a third-class lever.

Una palanca con el fulcro en un extremo y la carga en el otro extremo se llama palanca de tercer género. En este tipo de palanca la fuerza está en el medio. Una caña de pescar es una palanca de tercer género.

fulcrum
fulcro

effort
fuerza

load
carga

15

A jack is a tool used to lift up a car. A jack is a lever. The load is the car. The fulcrum is in the middle. A person uses the handle to lift the load.

El gato es una herramienta que se usa para levantar automóviles. El gato es una palanca. La carga es el auto. El fulcro está en el medio. La persona usa la palanca para levantar la carga.

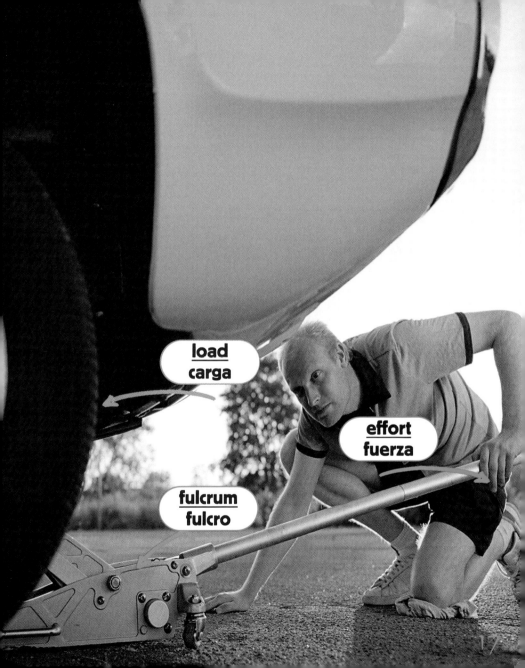

load
carga

effort
fuerza

fulcrum
fulcro

A baseball bat is a lever, too. Do you know why? The ball is the load. The person swinging the bat is the effort. The person's hands are the fulcrum.

El bate de béisbol es también una palanca. ¿Sabes por qué? La pelota es la carga. La persona que balancea el bate es la fuerza. Las manos de la persona son el fulcro.

effort
fuerza

load
carga

fulcrum
fulcro

Can you think of levers you see around you? Look at this picture. Can you find the lever here?

¿Puedes pensar en otras palancas que haya a tu alrededor? Mira esta foto: ¿puedes encontrar una palanca aquí?

Words to Know
Palabras que debes saber

effort
fuerza

fulcrum
fulcro

jack
gato

load
carga

Here are more books to read about levers:
Otros libros que puedes leer sobre las palancas:

In English/En inglés
What Is a Lever? (Welcome Books)
by Lloyd G. Douglas
Children's Press, 2002

In Spanish/En español
Palancas
Máquinas Simples/Simple Machines
by Michael S. Dahl
Bridgestone Books, 1999

Web Sites/En Internet
Due to the changing nature of Internet links,
PowerKids Press and Editorial Buenas Letras have
developed an online list of Web sites related to the
subject of this book. This site is updated regularly.
Please use this link to access the list:

www.powerkidslinks.com/mws/levers/

Index

Índice

Word Count: 295

Número de palabras: 308

Note to Librarians, Teachers, and Parents

PowerKids Readers are specially designed to help emergent and beginning readers build their skills in reading for information. Sentences are short and simple, employing a basic vocabulary of sight words, simple vocabulary, and basic concepts, as well as new words that describe objects or processes that relate to the topic. Large type, clean design, and stunning photographs corresponding directly to the text all help children to decipher meaning. Features such as a contents page, picture glossary, and index introduce children to the basic elements of a book, which they will encounter in their future reading experiences.